JOHN F. KENNEDY
OUR THIRTY-FIFTH PRESIDENT

by Judith E. Harper

THE CHILD'S WORLD ®

Published in the United States of America

The Child's World®
1980 Lookout Drive • Mankato, MN 56003-1705
800-599-READ • www.childsworld.com

Acknowledgments
The Child's World®: Mary Berendes, Publishing Director

The Creative Spark: Mary McGavic, Project Director; Shari Joffe, Editorial
Director; Deborah Goodsite, Photo Research; Nancy Ratkiewich, Page Production

The Design Lab: Kathleen Petelinsek, Design

Content Adviser: Celena Illuzzi, John Fitzgerald Kennedy National Historic Site,
Brookline, Massachusetts.

Photos
Cover and page 3: The Granger Collection, New York

Interior: Associated Press Images: 12, 15, 25, 33, 31 (HO); The Bridgeman Art
Library: 21; Corbis: 13, 20, 22 and 38, 23, 31 (Bettmann), 18 (Ted Spiegel),
36 (Tom Dillard/Dallas Morning News); Getty Images: 4 (Tony Tomsic), 10
(Hulton Archive), 26 (Getty), 35 (Keystone); The Granger Collection, New York:
5 (Gerhard-ullstein bild), 19; The Image Works: 8, 9, 27 (Topham), 29 and
39 (Berlin-Bild/SV-Bilderdienst); iStockphoto: 44 (Tim Fan); John F. Kennedy
Presidential Library: 7 (John F. Kennedy Library Foundation), 11,16, 28 and
39 (Cecil Stoughton, White House), 34 (Robert Knudsen, White House);
SuperStock: 17 (SuperStock, Inc.), 24 (Underwood Photo Archives); U.S. Air
Force photo: 45.

Library of Congress Cataloging-in-Publication Data

Harper, Judith E., 1953–
  John F. Kennedy / by Judith E. Harper.
      p. cm.— (Presidents of the U.S.A.)
  Includes bibliographical references and index.
  ISBN 978-1-60253-063-8 (library bound : alk. paper)
  1. Kennedy, John F. (John Fitzgerald), 1917–1963—Juvenile literature. 2.
Presidents—United States—Biography—Juvenile literature. I. Title. II. Series.

  E842.Z9H24 2008
  973.922092—dc22
  [B]

                                        2007049069

Despite John F. Kennedy's brief term in office, many Americans consider him one of the greatest American presidents.

TABLE OF CONTENTS

A BRIGHT FUTURE

On election night, November 8, 1960, Senator John F. Kennedy went to bed not knowing if he had won or lost the presidential election. It wasn't until nine the next morning that he learned he had been elected president of the United States. He defeated Vice President Richard Nixon by 303 to 219 electoral votes. The electoral votes, not the ballots of American voters, determine who will be president. The members of the Electoral College in each state cast the electoral votes for their state.

After Kennedy's victory, it took weeks for the popular vote—the votes of the American people—to be counted and recounted. Even though the popular vote does not elect the president, it is important. Although the members of the Electoral College are not required to vote a certain way, their votes are supposed to reflect the popular vote in their state. Kennedy was stunned to

At age 43, John F. Kennedy was the youngest man ever elected president.

learn that his victory was extremely small. Out of more than 68 million votes cast, he received only 118,500 more than Nixon. Kennedy received 49.7% of the popular vote, and Nixon earned 49.6%. The popular vote made the election one of the closest presidential races in U.S. history.

Kennedy's family was jubilant about his triumph, but Kennedy was worried. He had been sure of a larger victory. Yet nearly half of all voters did not choose him to be president. As Kennedy saw it, a huge challenge stood before him. He would have to prove to the American people that he was the best man to run the

John F. Kennedy was born in this nine-room, three-story house in Brookline, Massachusetts.

When he was almost three years old, John Kennedy fell seriously ill with scarlet fever and nearly died. He was in the hospital, away from his family, for more than three months.

John Kennedy loved to read. As a young boy, he enjoyed adventure stories and tales of fantasy. As a teenager, he chose books about history. He especially loved to read about famous world leaders.

country. He must work hard to deliver the promises he made during the **campaign.**

Kennedy's entire life had been full of tests and challenges. Even though he grew up with many advantages, life had never been easy. He overcame obstacles throughout his childhood and young adulthood. And when he made up his mind to do something, he did not turn back.

John Fitzgerald Kennedy was born in Brookline, Massachusetts, on May 29, 1917. He was the second child of Joseph and Rose Kennedy. Joseph was a wealthy businessman, and Rose was the daughter of one of Boston's best-known politicians. Both Joseph's and Rose's grandparents were **immigrants** from Ireland.

Joseph and Rose practiced the Roman Catholic religion. As Irish Catholics, they and their families faced the harsh **prejudice** of Protestant Bostonians. Rose's father, John Fitzgerald, and Joseph's father, Patrick Kennedy, did not allow the prejudice to discourage them. They worked hard. They also helped other Boston Irish families to get ahead. They achieved this goal by becoming involved in **politics.** John Fitzgerald was mayor of Boston and a U.S. congressman. Patrick Kennedy was a Massachusetts state senator. Through politics, these men passed laws and found ways to improve life for all immigrants.

As a child, John F. Kennedy—known to his family and friends as "Jack"—struggled to keep up with his brother Joe Jr. This was not an easy task. Joe was two years older. He was healthier, stronger, and

As a boy, Jack made friends easily. He was fun-loving and full of mischief.

more studious. Jack also suffered from many illnesses. Yet these differences did not slow him down. The intelligent, well-coordinated boy never stopped trying to beat his brother at games and sports.

When Jack was 10 years old, his family moved to the suburbs of New York City. His father believed there would be less prejudice there than in Boston. At age 14, Jack attended the Choate School in Connecticut. According to his teachers, he was not a good student. His schoolwork was carelessly done and did not show his true ability. He excelled in sports, however, especially swimming.

When he was very young, Joe Jr., Jack's older brother, announced that he would become president one day. The family thought Joe would be the politician in the family, and John would be a writer or teacher.

7

The Kennedys were a close-knit family. This photograph shows Rose and Joe Kennedy with all nine of their children in 1938. Seated are Eunice, Jean, Edward (on his father's lap), Patricia, and Kathleen. Standing are Rosemary, Robert, John, Rose, and Joseph Jr.

After graduating from Choate in 1935, Jack briefly attended Princeton University in New Jersey. A severe illness forced him to drop out, but in 1936, Jack followed Joe Jr. to Harvard College in Massachusetts.

In 1937, President Franklin Roosevelt appointed Joseph Sr. to be the U.S. ambassador to Great Britain. Living in England was an adventure for the entire Kennedy family. In the spring and early summer of 1939, Europe became Jack's classroom. He had two missions. The first was to gather facts for his **thesis,** a long paper he planned to write during his senior year at Harvard. To do this, he had to observe, take notes, and study how each European country was preparing for war. His second mission was to send this information to his father. Jack wrote to his father often while touring Europe. He described what was happening in each country he visited. Jack observed Europe at a crucial time—in the months before the start of World War II.

Jack began his tour in Paris, France, in April 1939, exactly one year before France was invaded by Germany. He spent a month at the U.S. Embassy in that city, making careful observations. He then traveled to eastern Europe: to Poland, Lithuania, Latvia,

Before Jack's graduation from Choate, his classmates voted him "most likely to succeed." This was meant as a huge joke because Jack was neither a good student nor a school leader. He was often in trouble with the headmaster and his teachers for playing pranks.

In the summer of 1938, Jack Kennedy (on the right) sailed to London with his older brother Joe and his father. In July, he worked with his father at the American Embassy in London.

Czechoslovakia, and Russia. From there he journeyed to Turkey and to Palestine.

By 1940, Jack's thesis was completed. In June of that year he graduated from Harvard College *cum laude* (with honors) because his thesis was so well done.

In 1941, Joe Jr. enlisted in the U.S. Navy. Jack tried to sign up, too, but his poor health caused both the army and the navy to reject him. For five months, Jack worked to make himself stronger. In September of 1941, three months before the United States entered World War II, the navy accepted him.

To Jack's disappointment, he was not assigned to sea duty. He was ordered instead to write news reports in Washington, D.C.

Jack said he worked harder on his Harvard thesis than anything else in his life up to that time. It discussed the reasons why World War II began in Europe. At age 23, Jack became an author. With help from a friend of his father's, his thesis was published as a book called *Why England Slept.*

Growing up, Jack always felt he had to compete with his older brother Joe. Joe was a great athlete, an excellent student, and their father's favorite son. When Joe joined the navy just before the United States entered World War II, John worked hard to strengthen his body so that the navy would accept him, too. This photograph shows Jack (on the left) and Joe in their naval uniforms.

In July of 1942, he enrolled in **midshipman's** school. There he learned all about the navy's **PT boats.** When the training ended, Jack was not sent overseas as he had hoped. He was ordered to teach men how to manage PT boats. He was extremely frustrated.

As would happen many times in Jack's life, his father asked his political friends to help his son. They managed to get Jack a combat assignment. In March of 1943, Jack arrived in the Solomon Islands, where he was commander of *PT 109*. There, in the South Pacific Ocean and its islands, the United States was at war with Japan.

Jack Kennedy (far right) and his PT 109 *crew*

PT 109

Life on a PT boat in the South Pacific was not very exciting. At least that's what Jack wrote to his sister Kathleen. Night after night, *PT 109* cruised the choppy seas as its crew searched for enemy ships. During the day, the men worked to keep the boat shipshape.

Then, on the night of August 1, 1943, *PT 109* was out on patrol. Its mission was to torpedo Japanese destroyers traveling nearby. The sky was completely dark. Suddenly Jack's crew spotted a destroyer racing toward them. Jack turned the wheel sharply so that the men could fire the torpedoes. But it was too late. The Japanese destroyer *Amagiri* struck *PT 109.*

The *Amagiri* was unharmed, but the crash split *PT 109* in two. Two men were killed. Jack severely injured his back. At first, the survivors clung to the wreckage. When rescuers did not arrive, Jack ordered his crew to swim to the nearest island, four miles away.

Jack took charge of Pat McMahon, who was too injured to swim. Jack clenched the rope attached to McMahon's life jacket in his teeth. He then swam to the island towing him. Once the men reached the island, Jack left them to search for U.S. ships. For days he swam from one island to the next, trying to find help. Finally, the native people of the South Sea Islands transported Jack and his crew to safety.

CHAPTER TWO

HIGH HOPES: THE YOUNG POLITICIAN

In 1944, Jack returned home from the South Pacific. The war against Japan would rage for many more months before the Japanese surrender in 1945. The newspapers declared that Jack was a war hero, but he did not feel heroic. He said that a commander's job is to save the life of his crew. He also said he did what any person would have done.

Jack was in severe pain from his back injury and he was ill from a disease he picked up in the South Pacific. He was very underweight and weak. But he was still able to joke. A newspaper reporter asked him, "How did you become a hero?" Jack said, "It was easy. They cut my PT boat in half."

The year 1944 was a terrible year for Jack Kennedy in other ways as well. He had a painful operation on his

*Lt. John F. Kennedy is congratulated after being decorated for **gallantry** in action in the South Pacific during World War II.*

In 1952, Kohei Hanami, the former commander of the *Amagiri,* read an article about Kennedy in *Time* magazine. In that article, Kennedy said that he had searched for Hanami while on a trip to Japan. Hanami was impressed that Kennedy wished goodwill to his former enemy. In a letter, Hanami told Kennedy that he believed the senator would encourage friendship between Japan and the United States, as well as peace around the world.

back that failed to help him. Worst of all, Joe Jr. died when his plane crashed in Europe. He had been on a secret wartime mission. Jack grieved with his family. In the following months, Jack dealt with his sadness by working hard to regain his strength.

A year after Joe Jr.'s death, Joseph Sr. decided that Jack should enter politics. As Jack later said, he had no choice. "It was like being drafted," he recalled. "My father wanted his oldest son in politics." With Joe Jr. gone, Jack was now the oldest son. According to his father, it was Jack's responsibility to carry on for his brother.

After much thought, Jack agreed to aim for a political career in Massachusetts. His family was firmly committed to the Democratic Party, one of the nation's two most powerful **political parties.** Jack and his father decided that he should run for a seat in the House of Representatives, part of the U.S. Congress. They knew it would be an uphill battle. Jack was unknown and had no political experience. Boston politicians said that the poor working people of his **district** would never vote for a "rich kid."

But Jack Kennedy proved them wrong. He never stopped campaigning. As long as there were voters to talk to, he kept going. In the primary election, he ran against nine other Democrats. In a primary election, voters cast ballots to decide who will be the **candidate** of a particular political party. Jack won, receiving 42% of the votes. This was a huge percentage in a 10-person race. In November, he easily defeated

Kennedy was not a skilled public speaker at the beginning of his political career. He found it difficult to talk to a crowd without a written speech. With careful study and practice, speech coaches, and talented speechwriters, Kennedy became one of the greatest public speakers of the 20th century.

the Republican candidate. At age 29, Kennedy became one of the youngest people to be elected to Congress.

Kennedy served in the House from 1947 to 1951. He concentrated on helping the people in his district. The lack of low-cost housing in Boston concerned him. He worked hard to make laws that would allow thousands of families to live in a house or an apartment of their own. He pushed for higher wages for workers. He also wanted the government to provide more aid to the elderly. He supported a **bill** that would permit immigrants from central and eastern Europe to come to the United States.

Kennedy was awarded the Navy and Marine Corps Medal for his heroism during World War II.

But Kennedy's work in Congress was not all he had hoped. He had little time to pursue what most interested him—foreign affairs, which are matters involving other countries. For this goal, he would need a seat in the U.S. Senate, which is the other branch of Congress. To prepare himself, he traveled 25,000 miles

From 1953 to 1955, Senator Kennedy was too ill to spend much time in the U.S. Senate. When he regained his strength, he made it known that he was fast becoming an expert in foreign affairs.

on a seven-week tour of the Middle East and Asia. "I was anxious to get some firsthand knowledge . . .of our policies in the Middle East and in the Far East," he said in a radio interview. He also said he wanted to discover what Americans could do to bring peace to Asia.

In November of 1952, Kennedy won a hard-fought campaign for the Senate. His entire family helped. His younger brother, Robert Francis Kennedy, was his campaign manager. "Bobby" was an excellent organizer. Like Jack, he had a powerful fighting spirit that never quit.

At the 1956 Democratic Party Convention, Kennedy became known to millions of Americans for the first time. The Democratic Convention is an important meeting where members of the party choose their presidential candidate. Adlai Stevenson was the party's choice that year. Kennedy almost

Kennedy's early years as a senator were difficult. He had the spirit and ambition to be a great leader. His health problems were the only thing holding him back, and this frustrated him deeply.

In 1953, Senator Kennedy married Jacqueline Lee Bouvier. Like Jack, "Jackie" was well educated, intelligent, and from a wealthy family. Jackie loved literature, music, and art. Jack Kennedy fascinated her from the moment she met him.

became his vice presidential running mate, but in the end was not chosen.

Kennedy became a member of the Senate Committee on Foreign Relations in 1957. He had long dreamed of winning this position. While on the committee, he strongly supported U.S. aid to poor nations in Asia and Africa. He also studied the spread of **communism** in Southeast Asia. He gave speeches in the Senate about the problems of foreign countries and discussed how the United States could help their leaders to solve them.

In 1958 and 1959, Kennedy worked tirelessly to help American workers. He pushed through a bill that increased unemployment insurance, which would help workers who lost their jobs. He also tried to make laws

While Senator Kennedy was recovering from back surgery, he began writing a book about eight U.S. political leaders who showed great courage. The best-selling book, *Profiles in Courage,* was published in 1956 and won the Pulitzer Prize in 1957.

Early in 1960, Kennedy decided that he must improve his public speaking. He worked with a drama coach. This specialist gave him lots of voice exercises. One routine was to bark like a seal for two minutes every day. Kennedy liked to do this while in the bathtub.

Senator John F. Kennedy shakes hands with a crowd in Seattle on the first day of his presidential campaign. People responded positively to Kennedy's natural warmth and charisma.

to stop the managers of **labor unions** from wasting the money of American workers. And in addition to all of his work in the Senate, he prepared to run for president in the 1960 election.

In 1960, Kennedy won seven presidential primary elections and lost three. At the Democratic Convention, he won the **nomination** on the first ballot. This vote made him the Democratic Party's presidential candidate. In his acceptance speech, he told Americans how his "New Frontier" program would improve their lives.

He chose Senator Lyndon Baines Johnson of Texas as his vice presidential running mate. Johnson was the powerful leader of the Senate Democrats. Kennedy selected him because he would capture the votes of southern Democrats, votes he would need to win the election.

During the campaign, Kennedy's religion concerned many Americans. After all, there had never been a Roman Catholic president. Some people said

The televised Kennedy-Nixon debates helped Kennedy in the 1960 election. Nixon, who was still recovering from a hospital stay for an injured knee, looked thin, pale, and nervous. Kennedy, on the other hand, appeared tanned, confident, and well rested.

that Kennedy might make presidential decisions based on his religion. They said they wanted a leader who would make the United States and its people his only concern. Wherever Kennedy campaigned, he said that his religion would never influence his decisions in the White House. He reassured people that he was not the Catholic candidate for president but the Democratic candidate who also happened to be Catholic.

Kennedy and the Republican candidate, Vice President Richard Nixon, participated in four **debates.** These were broadcast on television and radio. Both men showed that they were knowledgeable and intelligent. But Kennedy had one advantage: He was a natural on television. He appeared relaxed, confident, and in command. Many people say the debates helped Kennedy win the election of 1960.

After the first Kennedy-Nixon debate, most people who listened to it on the radio thought that Nixon won. Most who watched the debate on television thought that Kennedy won.

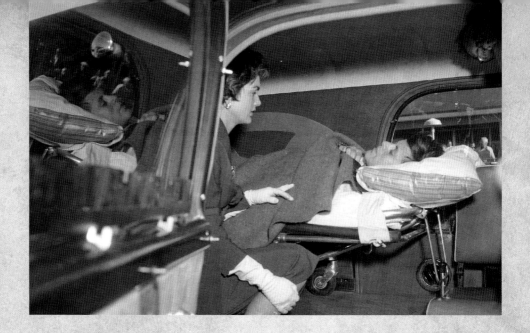

A PRIVATE STRUGGLE

During most of his years in Congress, Jack was weak, underweight, and exhausted. In 1947, doctors discovered that he had a serious illness called Addison's disease. There was no treatment or cure. The doctors believed that Jack did not have long to live. But Jack decided to keep working and hid the fact that he had the disease. He did not want people to think that he wasn't strong enough to handle his duties. This was important, because he planned to begin a campaign for higher office.

In 1950, doctors developed a medicine for Addison's disease. Jack felt stronger than he had in years, but the drug was not a cure. He struggled with the illness for the rest of his life.

As Jack felt stronger, his back pain became worse. He was often unable to walk without crutches. He needed surgery, but doctors warned him that it would threaten his life. Surgery was risky because of his Addison's disease. Jack wanted the operation. Only if his back pain were eased would life be worth living.

After the surgery in October of 1954, an infection spread through his body and he nearly died. With Jackie by his side, Jack began a long recovery. His back failed to heal, however. He risked another, more successful operation. In May of 1955, he returned to the Senate. He was finally strong enough to do the job. Unfortunately, he continued to struggle with back pain for the rest of his life.

CHAPTER THREE

THE CRISIS YEARS

Inaguration Day, January 20, 1961. Washington, D.C. was blanketed with eight inches (20 cm) of new snow. After taking the oath of office, President John F. Kennedy stood in the bitter cold and delivered one of the most memorable speeches in U.S. history. He was eager to begin leading the nation and was determined to launch his New Frontier program right away.

Kennedy's first presidential order sent food to poverty-stricken areas. With the help of Congress, he signed bills into law that helped poor working people. One law raised the minimum wage to $1.25 per hour. Another set aside government dollars to improve poor communities. Kennedy also succeeded in pushing through a multi-billion-dollar housing bill. This helped thousands of Americans to rent or own their homes.

Kennedy's wit, his ability to make fun of himself, and his hard work made him very popular.

As Kennedy was working to fulfill his campaign promises, the country faced one crisis after another. Suddenly the new president found himself involved in the worst crises of the Cold War.

The Cold War was not a war in the usual sense. No soldiers or sailors fought in battle. The Cold War was a conflict of words and threats between the United States and the **Soviet Union.** The Soviet Union was trying to spread its system of government, called communism, to other nations. The United States was determined to stop communists from taking over other countries. It helped **democracies** protect their governments from communism. It also encouraged other countries to become democratic like the United States.

At his inauguration, Kennedy began his 1,037 days as president by giving an unforgettable speech. With his famous words "Ask not what your country can do for you—ask what you can do for your country," he urged Americans to join together to work for freedom and lasting peace at home and around the world.

President Kennedy received much approval for founding the Peace Corps. This organization sends U.S. volunteers to help people in poor communities in Asia, Latin America, and Africa. Kennedy hoped that the Peace Corps would spread peace and goodwill throughout the world. Here Kennedy is shown congratulating the first group of Peace Corps volunteers in 1962.

In the spring of 1961, the president approved a new program called the Alliance for Progress. It offered help to the poor nations of Latin America, which includes Mexico and the countries within South America and Central America. The United States had a long history of paying little attention to the people of these countries. President Kennedy wanted to change that. He believed that if their problems were ignored, they might accept communist leaders and lose their freedoms. He also said that if these countries became communist, they might threaten our freedoms.

The Alliance provided loans of money to countries within the Alliance. They could use these funds for education, to develop industry, and to improve

Kennedy was a constant reader. He read at least four newspapers every morning with his breakfast. He read magazines as well. He also found the time to read three or four books every week. Kennedy was a speed reader. He once estimated that he could read 1,000 words per minute.

*Fidel Castro (on the left) became the leader of Cuba in 1959. In 1961, under his dictatorship, Cuba's government became communist. Here Castro is shown with his **ally,** Soviet leader Nikita Khrushchev.*

Joseph Kennedy Sr. suffered a series of strokes in December 1961. In his case, blood clots in his brain caused severe damage. From this time on, Joseph Sr. used a wheelchair and could speak very little. He was no longer able to help or to give advice to his sons. Joseph Sr. died on November 18, 1969.

farming. The Alliance was not a complete success, but the president refused to be discouraged. He believed that the United States must keep trying to help the people of Latin America.

Kennedy's first Cold War crisis was his biggest failure as president. In April of 1961, the United States began an invasion of Cuba, a small island nation near Florida. Cuba was ruled by communist **dictator** Fidel Castro. The Bay of Pigs invasion was supposed to remove Castro from power and end communist rule in Cuba. But the mission was a disaster.

Kennedy blamed himself for the failure. Military leaders and other advisors had told him that the invasion would likely succeed. Kennedy believed that he should have realized it would never work. He vowed to make decisions more carefully in the future.

Despite the disaster, Kennedy was convinced that Cuba must be freed from communism. It was too close to the United States mainland and too friendly with the Soviet Union for U.S. safety. Through a plan called Operation Mongoose, U.S. government agents interfered with Cuba's business with other nations. The U.S. Navy patrolled the waters around Cuba. The U.S. government also arranged to have Castro **assassinated,** although this plan did not succeed.

Castro grew alarmed. He believed that the United States was about to invade his country. He asked Soviet leader Nikita Khrushchev for help. The Soviet Union

Kennedy chose his younger brother Robert (at left), a lawyer, as U.S. attorney general. At first he did not want to select Bobby, but their father convinced Jack that he needed his brother. His father said that he must have at least one advisor who he could trust completely.

MEDIUM RANGE BALLISTIC MISSILE BASE IN CUBA

SAN CRISTOBAL

LAUNCH POSITION

MISSILE-READY TENTS

MISSILE ERECTORS

LATE OCTOBER

This once top-secret photograph, taken by a U.S. spy plane, proved that there were Soviet nuclear-missile bases on Cuban soil.

sent **nuclear missiles** to Cuba—weapons that could strike the United States. The building of missile sites triggered the Cuban Missile Crisis in October of 1962.

Kennedy knew that the United States could not allow nuclear missiles in Cuba because Cuba was so near to the United States. But getting rid of them presented a huge problem. If the United States entered Cuba or bombed the missile sites, the Soviet Union might declare war. Warfare in the 1960s was extremely risky. An ordinary battle could turn into a nuclear war. Such a war could destroy not only the United States and the Soviet Union, but other parts of the world as well.

For days, Kennedy and his advisors considered what to do. Finally, the president made his decision. He ordered a naval **blockade** of Cuba. This meant that the U.S. Navy would stop Soviet ships from delivering materials to the missile sites. Kennedy believed that this was the safest way to put an end to the crisis. He then demanded that the Soviet ships turn around and go home.

It was a terrifying time for the American people. What if Soviet leader Nikita Khrushchev ordered the ships to fight their way through the blockade? Would a nuclear war result? The entire world watched and waited.

Khrushchev ordered the Soviet ships to turn away from Cuba. He offered to make a deal with Kennedy. The Soviet missiles would leave Cuba if the United States promised never to invade Cuba and to remove its missiles from Turkey. Kennedy agreed. The Cuban Missile Crisis was over.

In the midst of these Cold War emergencies, another enormous struggle was heating up, this time in the United States. The **Civil Rights Movement** was gaining power. In much of the South, African Americans were protesting **segregation** and their lack of civil rights, which are the rights guaranteed to American citizens by the U.S. Constitution. Civil rights include the freedom to vote,

On October 22, 1962, President Kennedy appeared on television and solemnly announced that the United States would enforce a naval blockade of Cuba.

Jack and Jackie's children made the White House a lively place. Caroline was born in 1957, and John Jr. was born a few weeks after the 1960 election. The Kennedy family is shown here vacationing at Hyannis Port, Massachusetts, in 1963.

Redecorating the White House was a special project of Jackie Kennedy's. To furnish the mansion, she collected historic American furniture and artwork from all over the country. The first lady said that the White House belonged to the American people. She believed that they should have the opportunity to take pride in it and enjoy its beauty.

freedom of speech, freedom of religion, and the right to be treated equally according to the laws of the nation.

In 1961 and 1962, Kennedy respected the goals of civil rights leaders. But he did not want the rights of African Americans to be a big issue. His relationship with Congress held him back. After Kennedy's first few months as president, Congress would not pass most of his bills. The Republicans and southern Democrats in Congress joined forces to block the bills he hoped would pass.

Kennedy feared that if he strongly supported civil rights, he would never convince southern Democrats to pass his laws. Not only that, he was sure white southern voters would not vote for his reelection in 1964.

The disturbing events of 1962 and 1963 would force Kennedy to change his mind about the Civil Rights Movement.

THE BERLIN CRISIS

One major "battleground" of the Cold War was the city of Berlin. After the defeat of the Nazis in World War II, Germany was divided into two countries. One was the democratic nation of West Germany. The other was communist East Germany. The old German capital of Berlin—which lay in the middle of East Germany—was also divided in two. It became the West German city of West Berlin and the East German capital of East Berlin. West Berliners were left with a big problem: How could they stay a part of democratic West Germany while surrounded by communist East Germany?

East Germany also had a problem. Its citizens were escaping to West Berlin to find freedom and a better life. In 1961, the stream of runaways became a flood. To stop them, communist leaders ordered that a concrete wall be built between the two cities. East German troops patrolled the Berlin Wall to make sure that no one escaped to West Berlin.

East German soldiers then blocked the one free road leading into and out of West Berlin. Kennedy was determined to keep West Berlin a free city. He ordered U.S. troops to march on the road. The East Germans did not try to stop the U.S. Army, and the road remained open. The Berlin Wall remained, but West Berlin did not become part of communist East Germany.

On June 26, 1963, Kennedy visited West Berlin. More than half its citizens came out to welcome him. At the Berlin Wall, Kennedy told them, "Freedom has many difficulties and democracy is not perfect, but we have never had to put a wall up to keep our people in." The cheers of the crowd were deafening.

TRIUMPH AND TRAGEDY

In the early 1960s, the front pages of newspapers were full of stories about world crises that threatened international peace. President Kennedy had to spend so much time dealing with these problems that it was a struggle to keep pushing Congress to make laws to improve the lives of Americans at home.

Most history books say that the Vietnam War began in 1964, the year after President Kennedy's death. Yet both President Eisenhower and President Kennedy struggled to help solve South Vietnam's problems. While Kennedy was president, the government of South Vietnam was under attack. North Vietnamese communists wanted to overthrow the South and make Vietnam a united communist country.

In 1962, U.S. generals advised the president to send large numbers of combat troops to South Vietnam to help fight the communists. Without U.S. help, the military leaders said, the communists would take control of Vietnam.

President Kennedy agreed that the United States had to act. But he refused to send masses of combat

Jackie Kennedy was an extremely popular first lady. President Kennedy depended on her for her political know-how and her gracious manner with foreign leaders. In 1962, the president sent Jackie on a mission to India and Pakistan. In India she met with Indira Gandhi, who later served as India's prime minister.

troops. He told the generals that he did not want to rush the United States into war. He said he wanted to send money, military experts, and troops to help South Vietnam's army.

In the fall of 1963, a U.S. mission to make a stronger South Vietnamese government failed. South Vietnam was in more danger than ever. Once again, U.S. generals urged the president to rush combat troops to Vietnam. President Kennedy replied that it was important to wait. He said he needed to study the situation. On the night of November 21, 1963, he told his advisors to list every action that the United States could take in Vietnam. The next day President Kennedy was assassinated. It would be up to the next president, Lyndon Johnson, to decide what the United States should do next in Vietnam.

President Kennedy especially wished that the people involved in the Civil Rights Movement would be more patient. Kennedy had so many world crises

In 1962, Kennedy's youngest brother, Edward "Ted" Kennedy, was elected to the U.S. Senate from Massachusetts. At age 30, Ted became the youngest person ever elected to the Senate.

For his back pain, Kennedy received shots of a painkiller called novocaine five or six times a day. They were injected into his back. Kennedy did not care that the shots were extremely painful. He always felt much better for two hours after each treatment.

that demanded his attention. He was also struggling to push new laws through Congress, laws that would improve the lives of all Americans.

But the Civil Rights Movement could not wait. African Americans in the South had waited hundreds of years for their freedom—for the same civil rights that every white American took for granted. Civil rights leaders told Kennedy that waiting was not only impossible, it was unthinkable.

In 1962, James Meredith, a young African American, obtained a U.S. court order. It told the all-white University of Mississippi to accept him as a student. The university refused. Kennedy demanded that the school admit Meredith. He sent U.S. marshals to protect Meredith and to make sure that no one blocked his way.

At least 2,000 white rioters protested Meredith's presence. More than 160 marshals and several hundred people in the crowd were wounded. Two people were killed. Kennedy sent thousands of troops to keep the peace.

In May of 1963, civil rights protesters—including many schoolchildren—marched in Birmingham, Alabama. They wanted equal rights and an end to segregation. Even though the participants protested peacefully, the Birmingham police fought back. They used dogs and water gushing from fire hoses to attack the marchers.

In June of 1963, African American students were blocked from enrolling at the University of Alabama.

Once more, rioters threatened the peace. On June 11, Kennedy ordered U.S. marshals to protect the students as they registered for summer classes.

These events opened Kennedy's eyes. He was shocked by the racial violence and hatred. He was horrified by the cruelty of police. He realized that civil rights for African Americans could not be postponed any longer.

On the afternoon of June 11, 1963, President Kennedy told his aides, "I want to go on television tonight." At eight o'clock, he delivered his most stirring speech on civil rights. He told the American people that "this nation . . . will not be fully free until all its citizens are free." He said he planned to send a civil rights bill to Congress. This law would allow African Americans to be served in all public places—restaurants, hotels, theaters, and stores. It would end segregation in public schools. And it would make sure that all African Americans were permitted to vote.

The shocking events of 1963, including Birmingham police attacking peaceful civil-rights demonstrators with dogs and hoses, made Kennedy realize that he needed to send a civil-rights bill to Congress. Unfortunately, he did not live to see the passage of this important legislation.

Of all the character traits he got from his family, President Kennedy said that curiosity was the one he most cherished.

33

The prospect of nuclear war hung over Kennedy's presidency. In 1961, he said, "The weapons of war must be abolished before they abolish us." Here, during his final months as president, he is shown signing the treaty that was a first step toward this goal.

Kennedy made audiotape recordings of cabinet meetings, discussions with his staff, his telephone calls, and nearly every word spoken in the Oval Office. These tapes reveal the problems the president faced and the decisions he made. The tapes are stored at the JFK Library in Boston, Massachusetts, where historians and students may study them.

Kennedy knew that he was risking his political future. By supporting civil rights, he was certain to lose the approval of white southerners. He knew that he would have a tough time being reelected in 1964 without their votes. But he did not turn away from what he knew was right. He would see to it that the Civil Rights Act became law.

Kennedy said that the most important achievement of his presidency was the Nuclear Test-Ban **Treaty.** Years of hard work and **compromise** with the Soviet Union went into this effort. In the summer of 1963, the United States, the Soviet Union, and the United Kingdom promised to end above-ground and underwater testing of nuclear weapons. They agreed that they would no longer poison the air or the oceans with these tests. Starting on October 10, 1963, they would test nuclear weapons underground.

In late November of 1963, President and Mrs. Kennedy traveled to Texas. Kennedy hoped that the visit would encourage Texans to vote for him in the 1964 election. While riding through the streets of Dallas on November 22, two shots rang out and killed the president.

The entire nation was plunged into mourning. President Kennedy had been so full of life. He was always bursting with ideas for the future of the country. It was very hard for Americans to accept that he was gone.

Shortly after Kennedy was pronounced dead, Vice President Lyndon Johnson was sworn in as president. In the months ahead, President Johnson convinced Congress to pass much of Kennedy's New Frontier legislation. The most important was the Civil Rights Act of 1964. At long last, the United States was one step closer to Kennedy's dream of freedom for all Americans.

Millions of people all over the world watched President Kennedy's funeral on television. John Jr., who turned three years old that day, saluted his father's coffin as it departed.

WHO KILLED JFK?

Decades after President Kennedy's assassination, people still question the cause of his death. Many Americans believe that Kennedy was killed by one man, Lee Harvey Oswald. Others are convinced that his death was the result of a **conspiracy**.

What do the experts think? In 1964, the Warren Commission—the official government investigation—examined the evidence. They decided that Oswald fired the shots that killed the president.

In the 1970s, a startling discovery was made. In 1964, the Federal Bureau of Investigation (FBI) and the Central Intelligence Agency (CIA) had not told the Warren investigators all they knew about Oswald's life.

Why did they withhold evidence? At the time, FBI and CIA officials did not give information to other government groups unless it was necessary. They knew that their facts would not change the Warren Commission's conclusion that Oswald was the only killer. As a result, they did not reveal all they knew.

Americans were disturbed by the actions of the FBI and the CIA. Some people believed that they were hiding facts about Kennedy's death. In the late 1970s, a Congressional committee studied the assassination. The committee's report stated that the president was probably killed by more than one person. Since that time, many researchers have continued to study the evidence, but they do not agree. Some experts say that Oswald was the only assassin and others say that many people were involved in a plot. In 1992, a poll found that 75% of Americans believed in an assassination conspiracy. Even though many years have passed, the debate is as active in the twenty-first century as it was in the twentieth.

Lee Harvey Oswald (far right)

A NEW FRONTIER

John F. Kennedy was not yet president when the U.S. space
program began. Project Mercury—the mission to discover if
humans could travel safely in outer space—was already
underway when he entered the White House.

On May 5, 1961, President Kennedy watched television
along with millions of other Americans when astronaut Alan
Shepard rocketed into outer space. His historic flight lasted only
fifteen minutes before his Mercury capsule landed safely in the
Pacific Ocean. From 1961 to 1963, five more astronauts would
hurtle through space.

It was a day to celebrate. Yet President Kennedy was
concerned. Like most Americans, he was frustrated that the
Soviet Union had been the first nation to send a person into
space. In fact, Americans felt they had been falling behind the
Soviet Union ever since 1957. In October of that year, the Soviets
launched *Sputnik,* the world's first satellite.

Kennedy knew that NASA (the National Aeronautics
and Space Administration) had more space flights planned for
U.S. astronauts. He wished to encourage Americans that the U.S.
space program would not remain second-best for long. After
Alan Shepard's flight, the president gave a speech. He announced,
"I believe that this nation should commit itself to . . . landing a
man on the moon before this decade is out."

Time Line

1917
On May 29, John Fitzgerald "Jack" Kennedy is born in Brookline, Massachusetts.

1935
Kennedy graduates from the Choate School. In the fall, he attends Princeton University.

1936
Kennedy enrolls at Harvard College.

1937
Joseph Kennedy Sr. is appointed U.S. ambassador to Great Britain. Jack spends school vacations in London with his family.

1940
Kennedy graduates from Harvard College in June.

1941
Kennedy enlists in the U.S. Navy. The Japanese attack Pearl Harbor in Hawaii on December 7. The United States declares war on Japan on December 8.

1943
Kennedy arrives in the Solomon Islands in the South Pacific on March 28. A Japanese destroyer sinks *PT 109* on the night of August 1. At the end of December, Kennedy returns to the United States.

1946
Kennedy is elected to Congress in November.

1947
On January 3, Kennedy begins his two-year term as a member of the U.S. House of Representatives. In October, doctors in England discover that he has Addison's disease.

1948
Kennedy is reelected to Congress in November.

1950
Kennedy begins a new treatment for Addison's disease. In November, he is elected to serve a third term in Congress.

1952
Kennedy is elected to the U.S. Senate.

1953
Kennedy is sworn in as senator on January 3. On September 12, he marries Jacqueline Lee Bouvier in Newport, Rhode Island.

1954
On October 21, Kennedy has an operation on his back. Days later, he falls into a coma and nearly dies. A long recovery begins.

1955
On February 11, Kennedy has another back operation. In May, he returns to the Senate and is able to walk without crutches.

1956
Kennedy's *Profiles in Courage* is published in January. At the Democratic National Convention in August, he makes a bid for the vice presidential nomination. He comes close but does not win the nomination. He becomes known to millions of Americans when he gives the speech that nominates Adlai Stevenson.

1958
Kennedy is reelected to the U.S. Senate by the largest number of votes in Massachusetts history. He prepares to run for president in 1960.

1960

Kennedy defeats Richard Nixon in the presidential election on November 8.

1961

Kennedy is inaugurated the 35th president on January 20. He forms the Peace Corps on March 1. The Bay of Pigs invasion begins on April 17 and fails within days. On May 5, the United States sends Astronaut Alan Shepard on the nation's first manned space flight. Kennedy and Nikita Khrushchev meet in Vienna, Austria, on June 3 and 4. In August, Khrushchev orders the building of the Berlin Wall. Kennedy orders troops to safeguard the free road in and out of West Berlin. Late in the year, Kennedy orders troops, then called military advisors, to Vietnam.

1962

In February, Kennedy sends more military advisors to Vietnam. A total of 12,000 military personnel serve in that country. Astronaut John Glenn becomes the first American to orbit the Earth on February 20. On September 30, 2,000 rioters protest the presence of African American student James Meredith at the University of Mississippi. The next day, he is successfully enrolled at the school. The Cuban Missile Crisis begins on October 14 when U.S. spy planes observe missiles in Cuba. On October 28, the crisis is resolved.

1963

Kennedy travels to West Berlin and delivers a speech at the Berlin Wall on June 26. On August 28, more than 200,000 people take part in the March on Washington. The Nuclear Test-Ban Treaty goes into effect on October 10. President and Mrs. Kennedy leave for Texas on November 21. Kennedy is shot and killed in Dallas on November 22. Vice President Lyndon Johnson is sworn in as the nation's 36th president on November 22. On November 24, Lee Harvey Oswald, Kennedy's assassin, is shot and killed by Jack Ruby.

1964

President Johnson signs the Civil Rights Bill on July 2.

GLOSSARY

ally (AL-lie) An ally is a nation that has agreed to help another nation. Cuba was an ally of the Soviet Union during the Cold War.

assassinated (uh-SASS-ih-nay-tid) A person who has been assassinated has been killed by a murderer. President John F. Kennedy was assassinated on November 22, 1963.

bill (BILL) A bill is an idea for a new law that is presented to a group of lawmakers. Kennedy supported a bill that would permit immigrants from Europe to come to the United States.

blockade (blok-ADE) A blockade is a closing off of an area to keep people or supplies from going in or out. During the Cuban Missile Crisis, President Kennedy ordered a naval blockade of Cuba so that the Soviets could not deliver weapons materials to Cuba.

campaign (kam-PAYN) A campaign is the process of running for an election, including activities such as giving speeches or attending rallies. Kennedy tried to keep promises he made during his campaign.

candidate (KAN-dih-det) A candidate is a person running in an election. In a primary election, voters decide who will be the candidate of a political party.

Civil Rights Movement (SIV-el RYTZ MOOV-ment) The Civil Rights Movement was the name given to the struggle for equal rights for African Americans in the United States during the 1950s and 1960s. The events of 1962 and 1963 forced Kennedy to become involved in the Civil Rights Movement.

communism (KOM-yeh-niz-em) Communism is a system of government in which the central government, not the people, holds all the power, and there is no private ownership of property. During the Cold War, Americans feared that communism would spread throughout the world.

compromise (KOM-pruh-myz) A compromise is a way to settle a disagreement in which both sides give up part of what they want. The Nuclear Test-Ban Treaty was a compromise between the Soviet Union and the United States.

conspiracy (kon-SPEER-uh-see) A conspiracy is an action by two or more people to carry out a crime. Many Americans believe the plot to kill President Kennedy was a conspiracy.

debates (dee-BAYTZ) Debates are formal meetings in which two people discuss a topic. Kennedy and Richard Nixon participated in four debates before the presidential election of 1960.

democracies (deh-MOK-ruh-seez) Democracies are nations in which the people control the government by electing their own leaders. The United States helped democracies protect their governments from communism.

dictator (DIK-tay-tor) A dictator is a ruler with complete power over a country. Fidel Castro has been the dictator of Cuba since 1959.

district (DIS-trikt) A district is a small area. Some politicians did not think voters in Kennedy's district would vote him into the House of Representatives.

gallantry (GAL-uhn-tree) Gallantry is bravery and fearlessness. John F. Kennedy was honored for his gallantry in World War II.

immigrants (IM-ih-grentz) Immigrants are people who leave one country to live in another. Millions of Irish immigrants came to the United States during the 1800s.

inauguration (ih-NAWG-yuh-RAY-shun) A politician's inauguration is the ceremony by which they formally enter elected office. Kennedy's inauguration was on January 20, 1961.

labor unions (LAY-bor YOON-yenz) Labor unions are groups of workers who join together to demand better treatment. Senator Kennedy tried to pass a law to stop labor unions from wasting their members' money.

midshipman (mid-SHIP-muhn) A midshipman is a student in training at a naval academy. Kennedy enrolled in midshipman's school during World War II.

nomination (nom-ih-NAY-shun) If someone receives a nomination, he or she is chosen by a political party to run for an office, such as the presidency. Kennedy won the Democratic Party's presidential nomination in 1960.

nuclear missiles (NOO-klee-ur MISS-ulz) Nuclear missiles are nuclear weapons that are launched into space and then fall to Earth to hit their target. The Soviet Union sent nuclear missiles to Cuba in 1962.

political parties (puh-LIT-ih-kul PAR-teez) Political parties are groups of people who share similar ideas about how to run a government. The Democratic Party is a powerful political party.

politics (PAWL-ih-tiks) Politics refers to the actions and practices of the government. Kennedy's grandfathers were involved in politics.

prejudice (PREJ-uh-des) Prejudice is a negative feeling or opinion about someone without a good reason. Irish Catholics once faced prejudice from Protestants.

PT boat (PEE TEE BOTE) PT boats were small, fast torpedo vessels that the U.S. Navy used in World War II to attack larger ships. "PT" stands for "Patrol Torpedo." Kennedy commanded a PT boat in the South Pacific during World War II.

segregation (seh-grih-GAY-shun) Segregation was the policy and practice of separating Americans—white and black—into two groups, according to race. Civil rights leaders wanted to outlaw segregation.

Soviet Union (SOH-vee-et YOON-yen) The Soviet Union was a communist country that stretched from eastern Europe across Asia to the Pacific Ocean. It separated into several smaller countries in 1991.

thesis (THEE-sis) A thesis is an idea or argument made by someone. Some colleges require their students to write a thesis before graduation. John F. Kennedy wrote his thesis on the causes of World War I.

treaty (TREE-tee) A treaty is a formal agreement between nations. Kennedy worked out the Nuclear Test Ban Treaty with the Soviet Union in 1963.

THE UNITED STATES GOVERNMENT

The United States government is divided into three equal branches: the executive, the legislative, and the judicial. This division helps prevent abuses of power because each branch has to answer to the other two. No one branch can become too powerful.

EXECUTIVE BRANCH

President
Vice President
Departments

The job of the executive branch is to enforce the laws. It is headed by the president, who serves as the spokesperson for the United States around the world. The president signs bills into law and appoints important officials such as federal judges. He or she is also the commander in chief of the U.S. military. The president is assisted by the vice president, who takes over if the president dies or cannot carry out the duties of the office.

The executive branch also includes various departments, each focused on a specific topic. They include the Defense Department, the Justice Department, and the Agriculture Department. The department heads, along with other officials such as the vice president, serve as the president's closest advisers, called the cabinet.

LEGISLATIVE BRANCH

Congress
Senate and
House of Representatives

The job of the legislative branch is to make the laws. It consists of Congress, which is divided into two parts: the Senate and the House of Representatives. The Senate has 100 members, and the House of Representatives has 435 members. Each state has two senators. The number of representatives a state has varies depending on the state's population.

Besides making laws, Congress also passes budgets and enacts taxes. In addition, it is responsible for declaring war, maintaining the military, and regulating trade with other countries.

JUDICIAL BRANCH

Supreme Court
Courts of Appeals
District Courts

The job of the judicial branch is to interpret the laws. It consists of the nation's federal courts. Trials are held in district courts. During trials, judges must decide what laws mean and how they apply. Courts of appeals review the decisions made in district courts.

The nation's highest court is the Supreme Court. If someone disagrees with a court of appeals ruling, he or she can ask the Supreme Court to review it. The Supreme Court may refuse. The Supreme Court makes sure that decisions and laws do not violate the Constitution.

CHOOSING
THE PRESIDENT

It may seem odd, but American voters don't elect the president directly. Instead, the president is chosen using what is called the Electoral College.

Each state gets as many votes in the Electoral College as its combined total of senators and representatives in Congress. For example, Iowa has two senators and five representatives, so it gets seven electoral votes. Although the District of Columbia does not have any voting members in Congress, it gets three electoral votes. Usually, the candidate who wins the most votes in any given state receives all of that state's electoral votes.

To become president, a candidate must get more than half of the Electoral College votes. There are a total of 538 votes in the Electoral College, so a candidate needs 270 votes to win. If nobody receives 270 Electoral College votes, the House of Representatives chooses the president.

With the Electoral College system, the person who receives the most votes nationwide does not always receive the most electoral votes. This happened most recently in 2000, when Al Gore received half a million more national votes than George W. Bush. Bush became president because he had more Electoral College votes.

THE WHITE HOUSE

The White House is the official home of the president of the United States. It is located at 1600 Pennsylvania Avenue NW in Washington, D.C. In 1792, a contest was held to select the architect who would design the president's home. James Hoban won. Construction took eight years.

The first president, George Washington, never lived in the White House. The second president, John Adams, moved into the house in 1800, though the inside was not yet complete. During the War of 1812, British soldiers burned down much of the White House. It was rebuilt several years later.

The White House was changed through the years. Porches were added, and President Theodore Roosevelt added the West Wing. President William Taft changed the shape of the presidential office, making it into the famous Oval Office. While Harry Truman was president, the old house was discovered to be structurally weak. All the walls were reinforced with steel, and the rooms were rebuilt.

Today, the White House has 132 rooms (including 35 bathrooms), 28 fireplaces, and 3 elevators. It takes 570 gallons of paint to cover the outside of the six-story building. The White House provides the president with many ways to relax. It includes a putting green, a jogging track, a swimming pool, a tennis court, and beautifully landscaped gardens. The White House also has a movie theater, a billiard room, and a one-lane bowling alley.

PRESIDENTIAL PERKS

The job of president of the United States is challenging. It is probably one of the most stressful jobs in the world. Because of this, presidents are paid well, though not nearly as well as the leaders of large corporations. In 2007, the president earned $400,000 a year. Presidents also receive extra benefits that make the demanding job a little more appealing.

★ **Camp David:** In the 1940s, President Franklin D. Roosevelt chose this heavily wooded spot in the mountains of Maryland to be the presidential retreat, where presidents can relax. Even though it is a retreat, world business is conducted there. Most famously, President Jimmy Carter met with Middle Eastern leaders at Camp David in 1978. The result was a peace agreement between Israel and Egypt.

★ *Air Force One:* The president flies on a jet called *Air Force One*. It is a Boeing 747-200B that has been modified to meet the president's needs.

Air Force One is the size of a large home. It is equipped with a dining room, sleeping quarters, a conference room, and office space. It also has two kitchens that can provide food for up to 50 people.

★ **The Secret Service:** While not the most glamorous of the president's perks, the Secret Service is one of the most important. The Secret Service is a group of highly trained agents who protect the president and the president's family.

★ **The Presidential State Car:** The presidential limousine is a stretch Cadillac DTS.

It has been armored to protect the president in case of attack. Inside the plush car are a foldaway desk, an entertainment center, and a communications console.

★ **The Food:** The White House has five chefs who will make any food the president wants. The White House also has an extensive wine collection.

★ **Retirement:** A former president receives a pension, or retirement pay, of just under $180,000 a year. Former presidents also receive Secret Service protection for the rest of their lives.

FACTS

QUALIFICATIONS

To run for president, a candidate must

* be at least 35 years old
* be a citizen who was born in the United States
* have lived in the United States for 14 years

TERM OF OFFICE

A president's term of office is four years.
No president can stay in office for more than two terms.

ELECTION DATE

The presidential election takes place every four years on the first Tuesday of November.

INAUGURATION DATE

Presidents are inaugurated on January 20.

OATH OF OFFICE

I do solemnly swear I will faithfully execute the office of the President of the United States and will to the best of my ability preserve, protect, and defend the Constitution of the United States.

WRITE A LETTER TO THE PRESIDENT

One of the best things about being a U.S. citizen is that Americans get to participate in their government. They can speak out if they feel government leaders aren't doing their jobs. They can also praise leaders who are going the extra mile. Do you have something you'd like the president to do? Should the president worry more about the environment and encourage people to recycle? Should the government spend more money on our schools? You can write a letter to the president to say how you feel!

1600 Pennsylvania Avenue
Washington, D.C. 20500
You can even send an e-mail to: president@whitehouse.gov

BOOKS

Cooper, Ilene. *Jack: The Early Years of John F. Kennedy.*
New York: Dutton, 2003.

Hakim, Joy. *All the People 1945–1998.* New York:
Oxford University Press, 1999.

Hampton, Wilborn. *Kennedy Assassinated! The World Mourns:
A Reporter's Story.* Cambridge, MA: Candlewick Press, 1997.

Heiligman, Deborah. *High Hopes: The Photobiography of
John F. Kennedy.* National Geographic, 2003.

Sommer, Shelley. *John F. Kennedy: His Life and Legacy.*
New York: HarperCollins, 2005.

VIDEOS

The American President. DVD, VHS (Alexandria, VA: PBS
Home Video, 2000).

Biography: John F. Kennedy: A Personal Story. DVD, VHS
(New York: A & E Home Video, 2005).

The History Channel Presents The Presidents. DVD (New York:
A & E Home Video, 2005).

JFK: A Presidency Revealed. DVD (New York: A & E
Home Video, 2003).

National Geographic's Inside the White House. DVD (Washington,
D.C.: National Geographic Video, 2003).

INTERNET SITES

Visit our Web page for lots of links about
John F. Kennedy and other U.S. presidents:

http://www.childsworld.com/links

Note to Parents, Teachers, and Librarians: We routinely verify our Web links to make
sure they are safe, active sites—so encourage your readers to check them out!

INDEX